colorful gardening

perennials

colorful gardening

perennials

Timothy Leese

with photography by **Jerry Harpur** and **Marcus Harpur**

RYLAND
PETERS
& SMALL
LONDON NEW YORK

Senior designer	Ashley Western
Designer	Sailesh Patel
Senior editor	Annabel Morgan
Editor	Jane Chapman
Picture research	Mel Watson,
	Kate Brunt
Production controller	Patricia Harrington
Publishing director	Anne Ryland

First published in the United States in 1999 as
Designing with Perennials.
This edition published 2002 by
Ryland Peters & Small, Inc.
519 Broadway
5th Floor
New York
NY 10012
www.rylandpeters.com

Text copyright © 1999 Timothy Leese
Design and commissioned photographs © 1999 Ryland
Peters & Small

ISBN 1 900518 78 3

Printed and bound in China
10 9 8 7 6 5 4 3 2 1

CONTENTS

Gardening with perennials is now enjoying a renaissance in popularity.

Introduction

Herbaceous perennials—plants that die back in the fall, are dormant in winter, then spring up again the following year—have been grown in our gardens for centuries. During the great landscape period of the eighteenth century, they were grown, albeit out of sight, in the walled garden. In the late nineteenth century, the traditional herbaceous border became popular as an antidote to the elaborate and expensive plantings that had been favored earlier in the century. Fashions in gardening move slowly, and the great borders of the European country houses in the early 20th century gradually became common in smaller gardens, so by the 1930s even modest gardens usually had such a flowerbed, painstakingly staked, deadheaded, divided, mulched, and fed, just as demanding as the perfect lawn.

After World War II, with labor scarce and increasingly expensive, many large herbaceous borders were grassed over or abandoned, but the wheel of fashion has slowly turned and gardening with perennials is now enjoying a renaissance in popularity. However, a true herbaceous border is not a viable

Above left: **What resembles a tender plant for the greenhouse is the fully hardy** *Schizostylis coccinea* 'Major', **a long-flowering subject for an early autumn border.**

Above center: ***Doronicum pardalianches* flourishes in damp, shady places, the bright yellow flowers enlivening what might otherwise be a dank corner.**

Above right: **The pale blue flowers of** *Corydalis flexuosa* **'China Blue' are carried for weeks and weeks between late spring and early summer. The plant will thrive in a damp, shady spot.**

Left: **Delicate green and red bells dangle from the stems of** *Tellima grandiflora*. **The leaves form a neat clump and have good fall color.**

Left: **The striking pale pink candles of** *Eremurus robustus* **make a stunning display at the back of an herbaceous border. Found growing in semidesert conditions in the wild, these plants require full sun and free-draining soil.**

option for many modern gardeners. Even the most devoted gardener would find it difficult to keep such a bed well shaped all year round, let alone attractively colored. Do not be seduced by photographs in glossy magazines or newspaper articles that suggest leaving the plants uncut for the winter so you can enjoy the sight of morning frost on the seed heads and dried leaves. In reality, there are usually more wet and windy days during the winter months than there are clear or frosty mornings, and consequently, by the end of the winter, your border will be a brown, soggy mess, an absolute horror to clean up in the early spring. A true herbaceous border requires a great deal of hard work in return for a few months of pleasure. So in the modern garden, shrubs and trees combine to form the permanent nature of a garden and provide a background for an assortment of colorful perennials that bring drama and interest to the garden.

What is the appeal of perennials? They have many attractions. First, they are instant. It is not necessary to wait ten years for an herbaceous perennial to reach its full potential. In its first year, an aster or a Japanese anemone will reach its full height and flower, even though, of course, older plants will increase in girth and therefore provide even more flowers. Another advantage is that, by and large, herbaceous perennials are hardy plants, not as susceptible to the ravages of winter winds and cold as young shrubs. Tucked neatly into the soil, leaving nothing on the surface to be damaged by icy, frost-laden winds, herbaceous perennials will gingerly poke their new shoots above the ground in spring, then burgeon forth during the warm months. And last but not least, there is the benefit of their beautiful and varied

With perennials, color schemes can be created quickly and easily.

Right: **Although there is nothing here to jar or clash, these borders offer a casual** **mixture of colors, including pinky-mauve foxgloves and yellow violas.**

Be adventurous and mix plants that appeal to your sense of color and form.

colors. With perennials, color schemes can be created quickly and easily and, equally important, be dismantled and moved around if the color combinations do not come up to expectation. Instead of waiting several years before mistakes are apparent, they can be seen in a single season and adjusted accordingly.

Another advantage of gardening with these plants is that many perennials will happily increase themselves without any intervention from the gardener, either by prolifically seeding all over the place or by simply enlarging underground and throwing up more new growth as year succeeds year. As a result, it is not always necessary to purchase large quantities of any one plant. This is, of course, a generalization, as there are some plants that look better in groups from the start, but others, such as peonies, eventually make large enough plants to be left on their own.

Successful gardening with perennials does depend to some extent on understanding the conditions in your particular garden and then choosing those plants that will relish and thrive in these

conditions. But there are so many perennials that even gardeners with the most difficult and inhospitable conditions will be able to find attractive and colorful plants that will flourish in their gardens. To find out what will suit your requirements, it is first necessary to do a little research and then experiment. But to make life a little easier and to help you choose the right perennials for your plot, this book has been organized primarily by garden condition, helping the reader to choose plants suitable

for their yard. Other chapters are arranged by growing habit, allowing readers to choose perennials to fulfill a particular purpose or create a specific effect.

However, it is worth remembering that all gardens have their own climates, all gardeners their foibles, so do not stick to the accepted rules, but be adventurous and mix plants that appeal to your own sense of color and form. There is plenty of scope for invention in color schemes with perennials, and they will repay the attention paid to them.

Opposite: **Quiet colors show well on a sunless day. Here the impressive globes of** *Allium cristophii* **are teamed with old-fashioned columbines in crimson and white and euphorbias for a muted, soft-toned effect.**

Far left: **Ranunculi and columbines combine in this eye-catching study in red, white, and blue.**

Left: **Against a spectacular mountain backdrop, a long border of irises looks its very best in the morning sunlight. Irises respond well to such an open and airy situation.**

Above: **When the undeniably sensational black-eyed magenta flowers are over,** *Geranium psilostemon* **makes a handsome foliage plant with the additional bonus of red tints in the fall.**

Choosing perennials to suit the situation and soil of your garden is the key to gardening success.
Full sun is the ideal condition for the majority of perennials, so those fortunate gardeners with a
sunny plot will enjoy an almost limitless selection of colorful perennials to choose from.

SUNNY AREAS

Everyone has an idealized image of the perfect herbaceous border; a vista of varying colors, backed by a neat evergreen hedge and leafy trees, viewed across a brilliantly green lawn, the whole scene flooded with warm June sunshine. And why not? If given a choice, surely every gardener would plump for a sunny garden, or at least one that enjoys sun in some areas at some

time of the day. In fact, there are perennials for all sorts of garden situations, from great drifts of delphiniums massed in a sunny bed to two or three tiny tender gems carefully nurtured in pots. There are perennials for the tiniest patches, and those for which wide open spaces are required. Some love shade, while others will thrive only in the sunniest of borders. Perennials are

incredibly versatile plants. But there is no getting away from the fact that full sun is the ideal condition for the majority of perennials that are grown in the garden, and if you are lucky enough to have a sunny plot, you will enjoy an almost limitless selection of colorful perennials to choose from. There are sun-loving perennials in every color of the rainbow, offering the gardener an enormous choice of plants with which to color the garden. From subtle color harmonies to bold, gorgeous effects, perennials in full-sun plantings are guaranteed to bring excitement and drama to the garden.

To start the year, one of the first plants to flower in spring is the perennial wallflower, *Erysimum*. The old favorite here is *Erysimum* 'Bowles' Mauve', a winning combination of blueish-green leaves with spikes of pretty, deep mauve flowers. This not only flowers early, it continues to do so for several weeks. Plant three of these together in a generous, bushy clump, and remember to have two groups in the garden, planted two years apart, as, although very quick growing, this plant is also short lived, so it is important to keep the display staggered. There are a number of other erysimums appearing on the market now, many in bold, eye-catching shades of yellow and orange, or combinations of yellow and mauve, and the majority are very pretty and well worth finding space for in the garden. Their only fault is that they lack the heady scent of the annual wallflower.

Pushing through while *Erysimum* 'Bowles' Mauve' is already in flower are the sage-green leaves of lady's mantle, *Alchemilla mollis*. The velvety textured leaves are finely serrated around the edges, and they have the curious and attractive trait of retaining little pearllike drops of water at their center after rain. Alchemillas will not flower until midsummer, when they produce a froth of loose panicles of lime-green fluffy stars held on fine stems, which tumble all over the place when it rains but soon stand up again when the sun comes back out. Another early perennial is *Anthemis punctata* subsp. *cupaniana*, an attractive evergreen (or rather ever-gray) spreading plant with finely cut, almost silvery, aromatic foliage and a mass of white daisies on wiry stems smothering the leaves by mid-spring.

In early summer the columbines, also known as aquilegias, appear in their varied forms. The ones that are mostly grown in modern gardens are hybrids, usually with blue-green-gray foliage,

Far left: **Columbines do well in both full sun and dappled shade, and are an ideal choice for this garden, where the cheerful flowers thread their way through areas of shade and sunlight.**

There are sun-loving perennials in every color of the rainbow, offering the gardener an enormous choice of plants with which to color the garden.

Left: **The stately spikes of the foxtail lily (*Eremurus*) rise majestically above a mixed bed, which includes a colorful selection of irises, astilbes, and daylilies.**

15

the delicate leaves very finely divided, and the graceful spurred flowers carried on long, thin stems held well above the leaves. The wide range of colors includes yellow, purple and mauve, red, pink, and white, and often the flowers are in two tones. Any combination of these is fully acceptable, and, as even the darker shades are softly hued, columbines work well in many summer plantings.

Columbines are considered classic "cottage garden" plants, and campanulas, also known as bellflowers or Canterbury bells, also fall into this category. Although campanulas are just as happy in shade as in sunshine, they combine so well with sun-loving subjects, such as old shrub roses, that it is with sunny borders that they are most frequently associated. Campanulas vary widely in height, but the taller bellflowers are particularly imposing in the summer border. The spectacular *Campanula lactiflora*, with its large heads of soft lilac-blue flowers, is a cottage garden favorite, and there are also some hybrids available in richer shades, such as *C. l.* 'Loddon Anna' carrying soft lilac-pink flowers and *C. l.* 'Prichard's Variety' with flowers of deep violet-blue.

In late spring one of the earliest peonies appears, *Paeonia mlokosewitschii*. This is a beguilingly pretty peony with a name so unpronounceable that it is thankfully more commonly known as "Molly the Witch." The foliage is sage-green, and the single, bowl-shaped flowers are a delicious lemon-yellow with a central cluster of rich golden stamens. A good clump of this peony near the front of the bed is sure to look good after flowering, too, as the finely cut leaves are most attractive.

Columbines work well in summer plantings.

Above: **The flowers of columbines, including these double forms, are available in a broad color range, but all have an airy grace. Although short-lived, they will self-seed freely.**

Right: ***Campanula lactiflora* 'Prichard's Variety' carries its violet-blue flowers for most of the summer. It is somewhat shorter than the species, reaching a height of about 2½ ft (75 cm).**

Far right: **The blue bells of *Campanula lactiflora* rise above the stunning spikes of *Lupinus* 'The Governor', whose flowers are best cut back when they are finished to prevent self-seeding.**

Geranium macrorrhizum is an accommodating geranium that works well threaded through the border in early summer. It is extremely versatile and could just as easily be included in the chapters on ground cover, shade, dry and foliage plants too, so happy is it to adapt to most conditions. It has prettily scalloped large leaves, marked in red, which become a more pronounced red in the fall. In early summer the red stems carry pale pink flowers, slightly mauve-tinted, which in turn form spiked, deep brownish-red seed heads. This geranium, although quietly invasive, is never a nuisance, not having deep, questing roots, so if it crops up somewhere unwanted it can easily be removed.

The brick-red *Geum* 'Mrs. J. Bradshaw' and *G*. 'Lady Stratheden', a warm, rich yellow, are both ideal plants for the front of the border. The ruffled semidouble flowers are held delicately over clumps of green leaves. The early daylily *Hemerocallis lilioasphodelus* is another early summer-flowering yellow beauty. Finer in all points than the later-flowering daylilies, *H. lilioasphodelus* has grassy leaves and beautiful lily-shaped, lemon-yellow flowers on long leafless stems. It increases freely at the root, so leave it plenty of room to expand. Other daylilies, which flower from mid- to late summer, have been much hybridized in North America, and there are plenty of bold colors to choose from, mostly in tones of yellow, although there are some that call themselves red and pink, usually, however, with a yellow base to the tone. One of the most beautiful and reliable of the group is the clear yellow *Hemerocallis* 'Marion Vaughn', and there are several others available in shades of rich apricot and orange. Take your pick.

No summer border is complete without a lofty cluster of lupines with their magnificent, colorful spikes. Again, there are dozens of different cultivars covering a wide spectrum of color. The attractive, distinctive leaves are like miniature palm leaves and the curious pea-shaped flowers are borne on tall spires. Lupines look best when grouped in multicolored clusters. The Russell lupines are most commonly available today, the results of one man's lifelong dedication to this genus. Cut the flowers once they are over, as the effort of setting seed weakens the plant, and you may be lucky enough to have a record flowering if you give them this attention. All of them are sweetly scented, and their perfume is as redolent of early summer as the scent of lilac.

No summer border can be complete without a lofty cluster of lupines, with their magnificent, colorful spikes.

By early summer, the great bearded irises are in full flower. *Iris germanica*, the oldest known variety, has an abundance of gray-green leaves and lavender-purple flowers on stems about 3 ft (90 cm) high. As with the lupines, there is a vast number of named irises, and new ones come on the market every year. Of the old and reliable varieties, *Iris* 'Jane Phillips', about 3 ft (90 cm) high, is pale blue untainted by red, with the added bonus of scent, while *I.* 'Arctic Snow' is pure white, as its name suggests. Another old variety, *I.* 'Louvois', still holds its own in the border, with its curious chocolate-brown and maroon coloring, which combines particularly well with lemon-yellow and cream.

Oriental poppies also feature prominently in early summer, with their large, hairy leaves and tall stems bearing fragile, papery single flowers. Although commonly seen in orange-reds, there are now several available in pink and white, of which *Papaver orientale* 'Royal Wedding', white strongly marked in black, and *P. orientale* 'Cedric Morris', a pale dusky pink with a central black splotch, are two particularly attractive examples. Plant the poppies well back in the bed, as after flowering the leaves become limp and floppy and need to be cut back. As they take up lots of room in their prime, it pays to plant other things in front of them so the hole left by cutting them back is less apparent.

Come midsummer, the choice of sun-loving perennials increases dramatically. Most of the campanulas are now in full bloom, as well as the perennial geraniums, such as *Geranium endressii*, studded with dark pink blooms, and the *Alstroemeria* follow soon behind. *Alstroemeria* were once considered exotic and unusual, but in fact they are readily available and not difficult to grow if some care is taken in their initial planting. The *Alstroemeria* ligtu hybrids are a blend of pinks, yellows, and oranges, in both strong and more subdued shades, all blending together beautifully above the silky, gray, pointed leaves. Be warned—they will need support, as they tend to fall forward.

In the height of summer, the hybrid peonies, the double forms of which produce flowers of immense size crammed with silky petals, are invaluable in the sunny border. The old cottage peony, *Paeonia officinalis*, a satiny deep crimson, flowers early, with most of the others following some weeks later. The blowsy, ravishing, double pink *Paeonia lactiflora* 'Sarah Bernhardt' is extremely popular and reliable, and for a luscious cream color, the stunning *P. l.* 'Duchesse de Nemours', with its crinkled petals and delicious scent, is hard to beat. If you want a red peony, *P. l.* 'Karl Rosenfield' is an intense, opulent dark red, while the lavish blooms of *P. l.* 'Président Poincaré' are a gorgeous crimson. But

Above left: **Early in summer, the wallflower** *Erysimum* **'Bowles' Mauve' comes into flower. Here it consorts with** *Achillea* **'Moonshine' and** *Iris* **'Jane Phillips'.**

Above center: **The oriental poppy** *Papaver orientale* **has a brilliant, if relatively short, flowering time, while its companion, the white shasta daisy, is longlasting.**

Above right: **White flowers with a dark blotch at the base of the petals grace** *Papaver orientale* **'Perry's White'. The plants need neatening up after flowering.**

Come midsummer, the choice of sun-loving perennials increases dramatically.

for something exceptionally exotic, choose *P. lactiflora* 'Whitleyi Major', which has large, single, bowl-shaped white flowers enlivened by long, yellow stamens and reddish-brown foliage.

Echinops ritro, the blue thistle, is well worth growing in a larger border. It has distinctively shaped dark leaves and an abundance of steely blue thistlelike flowers, occupying 4 ft (1.2 m) of the bed in all directions. Another attention seeker is *Inula magnifica*, which grows to 6 ft (1.8 m) or more, and is an immense yellow daisy that is held above vast, mid-green leaves, a most splendid midsummer sight. Colorful and long-flowering, with pretty tubular blooms, penstemons are another valuable addition to the summer border. *Penstemon* 'Andenken an Friedrich Hahn', a flamboyant purple-scarlet variety, and *P.* 'Drinkstone' are among the better-known varieties. There is also a pretty, delicate pale pink and white variety called *P.* 'Apple Blossom', and another in palest mauve with the rather unappealing name of *P.* 'Sour Grapes'.

The fiery orange-red flowers of the perennial corm *Crocosmia* 'Lucifer' are a colorful late-summer sight. In intense shades of red, orange, and yellow, the boldly colored tubular flowers are carried on arching, elegant sprays among abundant

Left: **The globular blooms of the tall-stemmed** *Paeonia* **'Ballerina' mix well with delphiniums, which will go on flowering for a while once the peonies have showered the ground with their beautiful pink petals.**

Below: *Paeonia officinalis* **is an old cottage garden plant. There are several hybrids of it,** *P. o.* **'China Rose' being a particularly fine example.**

Right: **Bold colors can be combined to stunning effect, as here where the flame-red sprays of** *Crocosmia* **'Lucifer' arch over yellow** *Coreopsis* **and purple** *Verbena*.

The fiery orange-red flowers of the perennial corm *Crocosmia* 'Lucifer' are a colorful late-summer sight.

clumps of fresh green, swordlike leaves. It is best to give this attractive plant plenty of room—it is exuberant but elegant, and seen in its entirety, it gives a prolonged and dramatic show.

By late summer the Japanese anemones appear. Borne on tall, airy stems and flowering for a long period, these simple, saucer-shaped flowers come in cool shades of pink and white. *Anemone hupehensis* var. *japonica* 'September Charm' is warm pink, and *Anemone × hybrida* 'Honorine Jobert' is pure white. Both go on flowering for a good two months. There are also some pretty double-flowered Japanese anemones, including *A. × hybrida* 'Whirlwind', from North America, and *A. × hybrida* 'Königin Charlotte', which is pinkish-purple with frilly petals.

Another useful late-summer plant is *Aster × frikartii*. Like the Japanese anemones, it flowers for a long period, and unlike many of the New England asters, it is free from mildew. The lovely lavender-blue flowers, with their glowing yellow centers, are carried on branching stems above rough gray-green foliage. These valuable additions to the border appear reliably throughout the summer months and right into the fall. The named variety *Aster × frikartii* 'Mönch' is the one to look for—it has perfect blooms, is resistant to disease and requires no staking.

Finally, *Sedum spectabile*, the oddly named ice plant, is another staple of the late-summer border. It is a fleshy, succulent-looking plant, with fat blue-green leaves and stems, and the flower heads are made up of many tiny stars, forming a flat-topped umbrella of dusty pink, much loved by butterflies. *Sedum* 'Herbstfreude' has deeper, richer coloring and the same glaucous foliage. Sedums do need splitting from time to time, as otherwise the centers tend to fall apart, leaving a large empty space surrounded by flopping, lax flower stems.

SUNNY AREAS GALLERY

Acanthus spinosus

Height: 4 ft (1.2 m), spread 2–3 ft (60–90 cm); flowers in late summer; fully hardy

An imposing plant with dark green, shiny, spiny leaves. The flowers are borne on long spikes, also spiny, and are purple and white. It is well worth devoting some space to this plant as it is very handsome all summer. The crown may need protection in its first winter to allow it to establish itself.

Anemone × hybrida 'Honorine Jobert'

Height: 4 ft (1.2 m), spread 2–4 ft (60–120 cm); flowers in late summer to early autumn; fully hardy

This Japanese anemone is a white, single form, tall and long flowering.It holds its narrowish petals in an overlapping whorl. While enjoying sunshine, it shouldn't be allowed to dry out at the root.

Anthemis punctata subsp. cupaniana

Height: 12 in (30 cm), spread 2–3ft (60–90 cm); flowers from early summer to autumn; fully hardy

Finely cut gray leaves form a neat ground-covering mat from which pure-white daisies spring for many weeks from early summer. If the plants look a little mangy in the spring, dig them up and divide them. Invaluable as an edging plant, and for low walls, or tumbling over steps.

Anthemis tinctoria 'E.C. Buxton'

Height and spread 2–3 ft (60–90 cm); flowers in midsummer; fully hardy

Soft lemon-yellow daisy flowers are profusely borne above finely cut leaves. This profusion of flowers can exhaust the plant; remove them when they fade to encourage the plants to grow again from the base.

Aquilegia alpina

Height: 2–3 ft (60–90 cm), spread 12–14 in (30–35 cm); flowers in late spring; fully hardy

The deep violet-blue of these prettily shaped flowers goes well with white and gray. Although delicate to look at, they are sturdy enough and stand up well to bad weather. They are not particular as to soil type.

Erysimum 'Bowles' Mauve'

Height: to 30 in (75 cm), spread 24 in (60 cm); flowers from early spring to summer; fully hardy

The unusual color combination of rich mauve flowers above pewter-gray foliage makes this perennial wallflower a valuable addition to the spring border. Plant new plants every two or three years to ensure continuity, as it is not long-lived.

Geum 'Mrs. J. Bradshaw'

Height and spread 18–24 in (45–60 cm); flowers in summer; fully hardy

Semidouble scarlet flowers with slightly ragged edges are carried on rather hairy stems over deep green divided leaves which form a small clump at the plant's base.

Hemerocallis lilioasphodelus

Height and spread 30–36 in (75–90 cm); flowers in early summer; fully hardy

This is the earliest of the daylilies to flower. The lily-shaped clear yellow flowers are sweetly fragrant, and the lush green sword-shaped foliage is also attractive.

Inula magnifica

Height: 5–6 ft (1.5–1.8 m), spread 30–36 in (75–90 cm); flowers in late summer; fully hardy

This showy plant produces brownish buds carried on wiry stems that open out to reveal large shaggy yellow daisies 6 in (15 cm) across. The dark green foliage is rough to the touch but sets off the flowers well.

Paeonia lactiflora 'Duchesse de Nemours'

Height and spread 28–32 in (70–80 cm); flowers in early summer; fully hardy

An early-flowering peony of great beauty, bearing large fragrant, double blooms of pure white, crammed with a mass of silky petals. The attractive foliage is dark green.

Penstemon 'Drinkstone'

Height and spread 18–30 in (45–75 cm); flowers in midsummer to mid-autumn; fully hardy

Like all penstemons, this has a long flowering season, from June to September. The pretty tubular flowers, clustered on a slender stem, are a rich crimson shade.

Top left:
Penstemon 'Drinkstone'

Top center:
Anemone × hybrida 'Honorine Jobert'

Top right:
Geum 'Mrs. J. Bradshaw'

Above left:
Paeonia lactiflora 'Duchesse de Nemours'

Above right:
Hemerocallis lilioasphodelus

Far left:
Acanthus spinosus

Left:
Erysimum 'Bowles' Mauve'

Opposite page:
Paeonia officinalis 'China Rose'

There are numerous perennials that will thrive in shady situations, many of them with attractive, striking foliage combined with flowers in a range of pale, delicate colors. Even though some sites are more difficult than others, even the shadiest garden can put on a beautiful show.

SHADY SPOTS

The cyclamen
is clothed in the
most beautiful
marbled leaves,
no two the same,
for the whole
of the winter.

The term "shade" can be hard to define, and there are in fact several quite distinct shady conditions, ranging from permanent shade—the deep, dry shade under evergreen trees or beneath high walls—to the dappled shade beneath trees and shrubs, to flowerbeds that have sun for half the day. There are also seasonal variations—the ground beneath deciduous trees enjoys higher light levels when the trees are bare in winter, allowing many underlying plants to flower early in spring.

Perhaps the most problematic shade is the dense and perpetual shade cast by the walls of buildings in town plots and evergreen trees in country gardens. In such circumstances the problem is often compounded by the fact that the ground is usually dry and covered with debris—dust, dead leaves, and twigs. And, to make matters worse, such areas are often too sheltered to allow the rain to make much of an impression. The root-bound deep shade beneath trees is perhaps the hardest to deal with satisfactorily. However, the resilient *Euphorbia robbiae* will manage to cope here, its tough roots withstanding the worst conditions. The same is true of *E. griffithii* 'Fireglow', which has glowing, brick-red bracts with yellow eyes that will brighten up even the gloomiest corner.

Equally content with these difficult conditions is *Cyclamen hederifolium*. The cyclamen, after flowering in the fall, is then clothed in the most beautiful marbled leaves, no two the same, for the whole of the winter. These leaves can vary in size, too,

some being distinctly angled and shaped. They are a deep forest green, marbled with soft gray, gray-green, and cream in patterns that make us wonder whether artistic endeavor is really worth the effort when nature manages these things so brilliantly. The cyclamen does, of course, flower too, producing, after several years during which the corms increase, sheets of tiny flowers in pink, mauve, and white. All these colors will occur naturally even if you start off with just one plant. The flowering time is particularly useful, as it is late in the year, and the effect is uplifting as flowers appear in the shadiest spots at a time when most perennials are dying down for the winter.

The stinking iris, *Iris foetidissima*, will not only grow among dry roots and beneath walls, it will positively thrive there. Its common name comes from the scent of the leaves, which, when crushed, are supposed to smell of roasted beef—presumably not an acceptable smell in a plant. It has the advantage of being evergreen, with narrow, green strap-shaped leaves grouped in neat clumps, and it will seed itself with freedom. The flowers are not striking, being somewhat insignificant and a slightly muddy mauve color, but *I. f.* var. *citrina* has pretty, albeit discreet, yellow flowers with mauve-brown markings. However, the stinking iris really comes into its own in the fall, when the seed pods appear. These are really very showy, like fat pea pods split to show rows of bright, shiny orange berrylike seeds. Few plants cheer up a shady spot with such a blast of color.

Far left: **Found in moist woodland conditions in the wild,** *Euphorbia griffithii* **'Fireglow' looks particularly striking teamed with other foliage plants. The coppery red bracts are echoed in the ribs of the leaves.**

Left: **Care is required when establishing a group of the ivy-leafed cyclamen,** *Cyclamen hederifolium***, as there is nothing of it visible during the earlier part of the summer, and there is a danger that the corms will be inadvertently displaced.**

Below: **Shiny, bright orange seeds, well displayed in their pods, are the main attraction of** *Iris foetidissima***.**

The dappled shade cast by overhanging deciduous trees or low walls is not usually quite so dry and dark, and the soil generally tends to be better. Accordingly, the number of plants that will thrive in these conditions is greater. You can, when planting in shade, always dig in some humus anyway, which is a great help in getting plants established.

Anemone nemerosa, the common wood anemone, is one of the prettiest sights in spring. From early to late spring, the white flowers are most elegant, glowing prettily in a shady spot as they nod over the finely cut leaves. Wood anemones colonize quickly and are indifferent to soil type, although they do like slightly damp situations. There are a great many named varieties, many with flowers in delicate pale pink, blue, and mauve, but don't spurn the old-fashioned white ones.

In shady borders or on top of low walls or banks, the bergenias are invaluable. Their large shaggy, leathery leaves are evergreen, and in some varieties the leaves turn a rich bronze-purple shade in cold weather. Bergenias are extremely tolerant plants, enduring all sorts of conditions patiently and with very little diminution of their attractions, but shade, with a slight element of damp, definitely suits them best. There is a good number of named varieties. One of the largest is *Bergenia cordifolia*, the leaves of which usually retain their fresh green all year, and which bears good heads of mauve-pink blooms on sturdy reddish stems. There is also a purple-leafed variety, *B. c.* 'Purpurea', which has all the merits mentioned above as well as purple leaf color in winter. Another excellent variety is the white *B.* 'Silberlicht', which is slightly smaller overall than *B. cordifolia*, but every bit as strong and reliable—a really good plant.

Tellima grandiflora and *T. g.* Rubra Group are a pair of pretty evergreens, with delicate bell-like blooms that are greenish-white when they open but soon develop a faint pink tinge. Both are remarkably drought tolerant and will thrive even in dry, rooty shade. The leaves of *T. g.* Rubra Group will enliven any shady spot, being green at first, but with a red edge, and coloring up very well in the fall and winter.

Left above: **Tellima**
grandiflora Rubra Group can
be classed as a groundcover
plant, its evergreen leaves
displaying a pleasant rosy-
red tinge in the fall.

Left below: **The common white**
wood anemone has some
cousins in pink or blue, of
which Anemone nemorosa
'Allenii' is a particularly
handsome example, its lilac-
pink flowers bluer on the
insides of the petals.

Above: **One of the bergenias**
bred during the 1930s was
'Silberlicht', whose pure
white flowers are excellent
for lightening a shady place.

Right: **This dazzling spring**
display features the purplish
Bergenia **'Abendglut', yellow**
and gold tulips, egg-yolk
yellow primulas, and clear
blue forget-me-nots.

Left: **The filigree leaves of** *Corydalis flexuosa* **'Père David' take on a slightly reddish tint after the blue flowers have faded.**

Above left and right: **Hellebores are plants of captivating beauty for shady spots. The unusual and immensely varied flowers of the genus are a bonus to the leaves, which can be mottled, veined, toothed, or deeply divided. The lenten rose** *Helleborus orientalis,* **and** *H. foetidus,* **which has pale green bells flushed with purple, are both evergreen.**

Right: **The pendant bells of Solomon's seal,** *Polygonatum* **×** *hybridum,* **make a wonderful sight in spring.**

Depending on how much room is available, *Convallaria majalis,* the lily of the valley, will happily romp in a gloomy border or the shade of a wall. It could almost be included in the chapter on ground cover if it takes to your garden. This exquisitely pretty, deliciously scented woodland native has sprays of small, waxy, bell-shaped white flowers arching over oval green leaves. Do not bother to grow the attractive *C. m.* 'Variegata' in shade—the pretty, cream-striped leaves will revert to plain green if deprived of sunlight. Lily of the valley does not always wish to grow where you want it to, so it is worth planting a few clumps in a number of different places, and being content with the one that succeeds. If all your clumps succeed, you have amazingly green thumbs, and will have a problem in eradicating the convallaria.

Another smaller, clump-forming perennial is *Corydalis;* a dainty, pretty plant for a shady spot that does, however, demand a degree of moisture in the soil. *Corydalis flexuosa,* of which there are several named varieties, has ferny, delicately cut, slightly glaucous foliage and carries above the leaves beautiful heads of spurred, tubular blue flowers, which last for many months during the spring months. *C. lutea* carries slightly smaller egg-yolk yellow flowers that are the same pendant, tubular shape as other corydalis, but with many more of them per raceme.

Hellebores are also light-shade lovers, enjoying the leaf-mold and the slight damp that are typical of shady situations. They don't need the damp to survive, but it does keep them at their best. The hellebores are a complicated bunch, and there is constant confusion about their names, especially as there is a great deal of crossfertilization when they seed, which they readily do. But don't be alarmed by this, and don't be anxious if your seedlings are not identical to their parents; it is all part of their charm. *Helleborus orientalis* has the greatest variety of coloring—the wide, cup-shaped flowers range from white to deepest plum purple, and, best of all, they flower in winter, quite unaffected by snow and frost. Occasionally, when the winter is very severe, the thick stems become quite frozen and the plant brittle, but if left undisturbed it should not come to any harm. *H. foetidus* has beautiful foliage, the apple-green leaves cut and spiny-edged, fanned out like a miniature palm leaf. The flowers, held in sprays, are small, light-green buttercup-shaped bells, edged in maroon, and last for weeks and weeks. Only cut them down when there is plenty of new growth at the base, and when other plants are beginning to outshine them in early spring.

By mid-spring, *Polygonatum* × *hybridum,* or Solomon's Seal, as it is more commonly known, will come into bloom. It will illuminate even the deepest, darkest shade, and is always a pleasure to see, with its long, arching wands from which greenish-white bell-shaped flowers are suspended, elegantly poised along the length of the stem. From above each hanging bloom, the leaves arch in pairs, ribbed and pointed. It is of no use to plant this treasure grudgingly; you must be generous with it and strew it around liberally. The stems will grow in different directions and really show up against a dark background.

While on the subject of pale flowers against a dark ground, there are few flowers more evocative of early summer than those of the common foxglove. This is not really a true perennial, but it seeds itself so prolifically that it will continue to appear in the general area in which it was planted, thus reappearing year after year. The common foxglove, *Digitalis purpurea*, is bright mauve-pink and has its good points, but in a dark, shady corner, try instead to plant the white *D. p.* f. *albiflora*—its tall spires of creamy tubular flowers will gleam in a dark spot, creating a rather ethereal effect when seen from a distance. The truly perennial foxgloves are rather smaller flowered, but they also possess a certain understated charm. *D. lutea* has small flowers of a yellowish-cream color, and the whole plant is smaller, too, and more dainty, reaching no more than about 60 cm (24 in) in height.

Clematis montana is not technically speaking an herbaceous perennial, but can be viewed as such, as it dies away in winter only to reappear the following year. It is very happy on north-facing walls, with its feet tucked away into a shady pot or border, and in this situation will flower prolifically. A rarer and very beautiful clematis is *Clematis × durandii*. This is not a

Left: **Foxgloves self-seed generously, so it is worth keeping the white form, *Digitalis purpurea* f. *albifora*, separate from the type.**

Right above: **There are a number of cultivars of *Phlox paniculata* represented in this garden, including 'Fujiyama', 'Norah Leigh', 'Sandringham', and 'Tenor'.**

Right below: ***Digitalis × mertonensis* comes true from seed, but needs to be divided regularly to continue flowering really well.**

Remember that the lighter, clearer colors show up best and will need the contrast of some dark leaves.

rampant climber, reaching only 10 ft (3 m) or so. It has large, fresh green leaves, and large flowers of a beautiful intense violet hue. *C. × durandii* comes into bloom in the very height of summer and will flower all the way through until the first frosts. It doesn't necessarily need a wall, as it can be trained through another plant, such as *Cornus alba* 'Elegantissima', where the rich colors of the clematis flowers will show up vividly against the cream-edged dogwood leaves.

If you are fortunate enough to have good moist soil beneath a deciduous tree, then *Trillium* is a beauty. It is a member of the lily family from North America. The leaves all grow from the base horizontally, and the flowers, of three petals each, have recurved petals and sit low on the leaves. *Trillium grandiflorum*, the best known of the group, is also the largest, and is a reliable and excellent plant. The flowers are usually a pure white, although there is also a pink form. The showy flowers, with their wavy-edged petals rising serenely above dark green leaves, make an extremely pretty sight in early spring.

Phlox has always been a colorful staple of the herbaceous border. In fact, it has a tendency to look pinched and dried-up in too sunny a spot and does much better in light shade, with some moisture at the roots. The phlox mostly used today are the hybrids of *Phlox paniculata*, with broad, densely packed flowerheads in a variety of colors, the leggy plants being often 4 ft (1.2 m) or so high. *P. paniculata* 'Sandringham', which is clear pink with a contrasting darker eye, is a good form, as is *P. p* 'Fujiyama' which is pure, clean white. It is a native of from the United States and has the added bonus of flowering in late summer, after most of the other phlox have finished their display.

One of the most important things to remember when choosing perennials for a shady spot is that lighter, clearer colors show up best and will need the contrast of some dark leaves or a dark background to look most effective. Deep or muddy colors are inclined to get lost in a shady position, so are best used on a small scale where they can be viewed close up instead of seen across a stretch of flowerhead or expanse of lawn.

SHADY SPOTS GALLERY

Bergenia 'Abendglut'

Height: 8–12 in (20–30 cm), spread: 18–24 in (45–60 cm); flowers in mid-spring; fully hardy

The leaves of this *Bergenia* are glossy apple-green, very fresh-looking, in early summer, then turn a rich reddish-maroon in winter, especially on the reverse. The semi-double flowers are a vivid magenta.

Clematis × durandii

Height: 3–6 ft (90 cm–2 m), spread: 3 ft (90 cm); flowers in summer; fully hardy

This is an excellent candidate for a shady wall, but can also be encouraged to grow through other plants in the border. It does not reach great heights, but the leaves and rich indigo single flowers, with their golden anthers, are a good size.

Corydalis flexuosa 'Père David'

Height: 8–12 in (20–30 cm), spread: 8 in (20 cm); flowers in late spring to summer; fully hardy

This dainty little plant has finely cut leaves, rather like the lime-green ferns to be found for sale in florists' shops, and its intricate

spurred tubular flowers are clear, bright blue. The foliage is dark and richly tinted with bronze and purple tones, showing up the blue flowers very well. This is a useful as well as lovely plant, flowering for a good two months throughout the late spring and early summer months.

Digitalis purpurea f. albiflora

Height: 3–6 ft (90–180 cm), spread: 18–24 in (45–60 cm); flowers in summer; fully hardy

Technically, *Digitalis*, or foxgloves, are not herbaceous perennials, but they self-seed so prolifically that they can justifiably be included here. This white foxglove is a stunning sight in a shady spot, the white spires gleaming magically in the gloom. The basal leaves need plenty of space to flourish.

Euphorbia palustris

Height and spread: 3 ft (90 cm); flowers in spring; fully hardy

Not an easy plant to track down, although it is well worth the search. The bracts, which, with euphorbias, pass as the flowers, are

bright acid-green in late spring, and very striking. In autumn the foliage develops tints of yellow and orange.

Helleborus × sternii

Height: 14 in (35 cm), spread: 12 in (30 cm); flowers from late winter to early spring; fully hardy

Distinctively colored flowers, in pale shades of green suffused with rosy pink, distinguish these hellebores from the rest. Some of them have beautifully marbled leaves. Remarkable and exciting plants, but unfortunately not suitable for deep shade.

Hosta crispula

Height: 20 in (50 cm), spread: 3 ft (90 cm); flowers in early summer; fully hardy

There is an enormous number of hostas available. In North America they are often grown for their flowers, in England for their attractive leaves. This one has white-edged undulating leaves, which are both long and large, and lilac flowers that appear in June. Better in clumps, where it is more spectacular, than as a specimen plant.

Iris foetidissima var. citrina

Height: 18–24 in (45–60 cm), spread: 1–2 ft (30–60 cm); flowers in early summer; fully hardy

Another plant that could not be described as a garden-center staple, but one that is worth searching out. This iris has greenish-yellow flowers marked with purple, but they are not very significant. The plant's most exciting contribution to the shady bed is the pods of plump orange seeds produced in winter, which will enliven the dreariest corner. The plant will even grow where you despair of anything else managing to survive.

Trillium grandiflorum

Height and spread: 12–18 in (30–45 cm); flowers in late spring to early summer; fully hardy

These attractive woodland plants have pure white three-petaled flowers that sit in a stately fashion above a mound of three dark-green leaves. The showy blooms have delicately waved edges. They will thrive in a shady spot on moist soil with plenty of leafmold, as it will remind them agreeably of their native habitat.

Above left: **Corydalis flexuosa 'Père David'**

Above right: **Helleborus × sternii**

Right: **Trillium grandiflorum**

Far right: **Euphorbia palustris**

Below left: **Clematis × durandii**

Below center: **Iris foetidissima var. citrina**

Below right: **Hosta crispula**

Opposite page: **Helleborus orientalis**

Gardens with naturally moist soil can play host to a wide range of colorful perennials, many of them characterized by their lush green foliage. If you do not have a damp garden, a man-made water feature will also offer opportunities for introducing the plants discussed in this chapter.

DAMP CONDITIONS

Left: **Primulas, including the pink- flushed** *P. japonica*, **the coppery orange** *P. aurantiaca*, **and the sweetly scented** *P. florindae*, **inject notes of color to this lush waterside planting, which also includes hostas, irises, and water lilies.**

Right: **Pink lythrums and orange crocosmias are excellent companions for the moisture-loving astilbes with their plumelike panicles.**

Below: *Iris ensata* **is a waterside iris, rather than one wishing to have its feet fully covered, bearing purple flowers that appear from early to mid-summer. The plant needs to be kept well away from limy soil.**

ground that surrounds a pond or stream. Fortunately, both types of damp ground are usually very fertile, and these environments will support a number of fine perennials.

True damp, such as a stream that runs even in a drought or a pond that is spring-fed, is a luxury in most of our yards, in which water, if there is any, is either artificially introduced or inclined to dry out in midsummer. If you are fortunate enough to have an ideal watery spot, then there are a number of plants that will flourish with wet at the root. Astilbes are perfect plants for this type of damp ground. They have finely cut, feathery foliage, which is often a coppery shade in the spring months. The pink- and red-flowering astilbes have the most colorful foliage—the pretty, lacy, white-flowering varieties have green leaves only. Astilbes are truly hardy plants, thriving in the sunshine as long as the ground they are in remains wet; half-shade is preferable if the ground tends to dry out a bit. There are many named hybrids to choose from. *Astilbe* 'Straussenfeder' has great arching plumes, some 3 ft (90 cm) high, in a delicate coral pink. One of the most decorative white varieties is *A.* 'Deutschland', with its bright grass-green leaves and tall sprays of creamy white flowers. There are also several dwarf varieties available, which can be planted at the edge of a stream or bank of a pond.

There are also several irises that will thrive in permanently boggy, damp soil. *Iris laevigata*, with its bladelike green leaves, carries wide-petaled flowers of soft lavender-blue in mid-summer, while *I. I.* 'Alba' has white flowers and *I. I.* 'Variegata' has broad leaves vertically striped with green and cream. *I. ensata* also enjoys watery conditions and comes in a variety of colors, varying from a deep purple to rosy pink and dusty mauve.

For a really exotic and spectacular sight, the vast rhubarb-like leaves of *Gunnera manicata*, with bristly ginger-colored fur covering the crowns, cannot be beaten. This giant waterside perennial has leaves that can reach 6 ft (1.8 m) across and will add a touch of the tropics to any garden, but be warned—they demand constantly damp conditions and take up a prodigious amount of space. *Rodgersia* is a slightly smaller alternative and makes an equally attractive architectural addition to damp areas. It reaches up to some 4 ft (1.2 m) in height, and in addition to its handsome and large leaves, it carries fluffy, astilbelike plumes of flowers in warm cream or bright pink.

There are also several irises that thrive in permanently boggy and damp soil.

As is often the case in a book about plants, there is inevitably a lot of overlap. In the plant world, hard-and-fast rules do not often apply, with the result that certain plants will thrive in several different conditions, perhaps preferring one of them, but still flowering happily enough in the others. Therefore, damp conditions will support some plants that also thrive in shade and others that will flourish in sun. In addition, some plants that don't actually need to be damp do better when they are, making the choice of plants for this condition even larger.

There are two different types of damp ground. The first is ground that is made up of heavy clay soil that does not drain well and therefore retains a great deal of moisture, giving rise to damp conditions. The second kind is true damp—the boggy, marshy

For areas that are damp rather than completely boggy, *Iris setosa* is ideal. This iris flourishes in the damp, and its delicately pretty deep blue-purple flowers appear in summer. *Primula florindae*, the giant cowslip, is also excellently suited to damp ground. Its leaves are short and round, and the numerous flowers, held on tall, straight stems, are a clear lemon-yellow shade, slightly deeper in color than those of the primrose. *P. japonica* is one of a large group of candelabra primulas, the colors of which are many and various. The plants have whorls of red or white flowers rising in tiers up the height of the stem. *P. japonica* can look particularly beautiful when grown in large quantities along the banks of a stream.

Schizostylis, the kaffir lily, seems an unlikely moisture-loving plant because it resembles something exotic, delicate, and sun-nurtured. However, in the wild it is usually found growing near streams and will thrive in damp ground. It has the added bonus of flowering late, bringing a welcome splash of color to the yard in late summer and early fall. *S. coccinea* 'Major' has starry flowers of a vibrant crimson hue borne on slender stems and opens a little earlier than the equally good *S. c.* 'Mrs. Hegarty', which is luscious pale pink. *Schizostylis* can grow up to 24–30 in (60–75 cm) in height, its long stems sometimes tending to flop a bit, but still looking as elegant as ever.

Perhaps the most obvious contender for damp, shady places is the fern, which can loosely be described as an herbaceous perennial as it vanishes from above ground in winter, although there are some evergreen varieties. Their splendid feathery foliage, in various shades of green, combines attractively with other foliage plants and acts as a foil for flowering plants. Try *Osmunda regalis*, the royal fern; *Athyrium filix-femina*, the lady fern; or *Matteuccia struthiopteris*, the shuttlecock fern, all of which will flourish in damp shade. *Dryopteris affinis*, the scaly male fern, demands damp soil, but will also tolerate a sunny spot.

For something a little unusual, try *Ligularia przewalskii*. These eye-catching perennials have clear yellow flowers clustered around tall, spectacular, ebony-stemmed spikes. The flowers are in striking contrast to the deeply cut dark green leaves. These are tall plants, reaching between 5–6 ft (1.5–1.8 m) in height. Their slender forms and bold flowers are elegant, and they combine well with *Primula japonica* and the powerful shapes of ferns.

For damp rather than wet areas, there is greater choice.

Left: **The impressive hosta leaves provide a wonderful foil for the colorful, moisture-loving candelabra primulas dotted along the bank of a stream.**

Right: **Grouping plants of the same color can be very effective. In this yellow scheme, the flowers have contrasting shapes, from the flattish heads of the** Achillea **to the curious spikes of** Ligularia przewalskii**.**

Far right, above: **Native to southern Africa, the kaffir lily,** Schizostylis coccinea **'Major', is vulnerable to drying out and will produce its finest display of flowers in an open, sunny spot in moist soil.**

Far right, below: **The airy, mauve-pink clusters of the meadow rue** Thalictrum aquilegiifolium **are offset by the exquisite irises in the foreground.**

There are many plants that, although not demanding damp or constant moisture, are undoubtedly happier in such conditions. *Thalictrum*, with its lacy foliage and fluffy pink, purple and white flowerheads, falls into this category, as does *Eupatorium ligustrinum*. This glossy-leaved evergreen has white or rose-tinted flower heads composed of tiny star-shaped flowers, and the whole plant is smaller and more compact than *E. purpureum*, or Joe Pye weed, which will also flourish on moisture-retentive soil, and has the added bonus of quickly filling spaces.

DAMP CONDITIONS GALLERY

Astilbe × arendsii 'Amethyst'

Height and spread: 2–3 ft (60–90 cm); flowers in early to mid-summer; fully hardy

An early-flowering *Astilbe* with open sprays of feathery flowers in a particularly clear lilac-pink shade, waving over finely cut, almost fernlike leaves. The new foliage, in common with other astilbes, is bronze-tinted with crimson undertones, and there is a similar mahogany tone to the winter stems and seed heads. As long as it is planted in moisture-retaining soil, this plant will be happy in either sun or light shade.

Cimicifuga racemosa

Height: 4–6 ft (1.2–1.8 m), spread: 2–3 ft (60–90 cm); flowers in mid- to late summer; fully hardy

You may have to hunt for this moisture-loving plant, but it is worth the effort. The leaves are a good apple-green and finely divided. In midsummer fluffy white bottlebrushlike flowers are produced, similar to some of the hebes, but carried on taller flower stems. Cimicifugas are at their happiest in light shade.

Gunnera manicata

Height: 6–8 ft (1.8–2.5 m), spread: 8–12 ft (2.5–3.7 m); flowers early summer; half hardy

This is an exceptional plant for a damp place, particularly when it is grown by a stream and its vast leaves reach up to become level with the steep banks. Although it is very large, it is so remarkably handsome that it is worth finding space for this elephantine plant. The coarse, leathery green leaves, which sometimes reach as much as 6 ft (1.8 m) across, are prominently veined and covered with bristles. The flowers are drab green, held in loose panicles above the toothed leaves. Protecting the crowns in winter is advisable.

Ligularia dentata 'Desdemona'

Height: 3 ft (90 cm), spread 30–36 in (75–90 cm); flowers midsummer to early autumn; fully hardy

A handsome plant that will bring a touch of cheerful color to a shady, damp bed. It has yellowish-orange daisy-shaped flowers carried on sturdy stems over large, green, heart-shaped leaves, the undersides of which are a dark reddish-brown. To put on a good show, it needs to have its feet very wet, especially if planted in a sunny spot.

Lysimachia ephemerum

Height: 3 ft (90 m), spread: 12 in (30 cm); flowers in early and midsummer; fully hardy

Lysimachia doesn't need to be drenchingly wet, but is happiest in a sunny place with a little moisture at its roots. It produces slender spires densely packed with tiny white flowers, which are set off well by the gray-blue foliage. It can be invasive.

Monarda 'Croftway Pink'

Height: 2–3 ft (60–90 cm), spread: 14–20 in (35–50 cm); flowers from summer and early autumn; fully hardy

Monarda, the hardy bergamot, is a prime candidate for a sunny but damp spot. The flowers, which appear in summer, are long-petaled and held well apart, forming a shaggy circle of strong pink, curved and pointed blooms. The foliage is neatly pointed and aromatic when crushed.

Schizostylis coccinea 'Major'

Height: 2 ft (60 cm), spread: 12 in (30 cm); flowers in autumn; fully hardy

In moist soil, the rhizomatous roots of this long-flowering perennial form large clumps of prominently ribbed, swordlike, light green leaves. The cultivar 'Major' produces large, exotic-looking scarlet flowers carried on long, arching stems; the blooms are star-shaped, and the petals have a glossy, satiny texture. The flowers are good for cutting. An open, sunny position close to water is perfect for *Schizostylis*.

Trollius europaeus 'Superbus'

Height: 32 in (80 cm), spread: 18 in (45 cm); flowers in early and midsummer; fully hardy

T. europaeus, the globe flower, is happy to grow in permanently wet ground. *T. e.* 'Superbus' produces a mass of perfectly formed spherical cups of lemon yellow carried over deeply divided fresh green leaves. It increases gradually and is particularly beautiful when it forms a carpet of yellow orbs.

Above: **Gunnera manicata**

Above center: **Troillius europaeus**

Above far right: **Ligularia dentata 'Desdemona'**

Below: **Astilbe × arendsii 'Amethyst'**

Below center: **Cimicifuga racemosa**

Below far right: **Schizostylis coccinea 'Major'**

Opposite page: **Ligularia hodgsonii**

Enlisting plants that thrive even when water is at a premium is the secret to successful gardening in dry, arid conditions. There are a whole host of drought-tolerant perennials that can be called into service to transform a potentially difficult area into a flourishing and colorful oasis.

DRY SITES

Right: **Plantings of *Iris pseudacorus*, *Euphorbia characias*, perennial geraniums, helichrysums, *Ballota pseudodictamnus*, and martagon lilies add subtle splashes of color that are easy on the eye so near to the house.**

Far right: **A mound of the wooly-leafed *Ballota pseudodictamnus* will thrive in poor, dry soil. Cut the stems off in August before they go brown.**

Below: **Clumps of just one or two varieties can be visually arresting. Here *Dianthus* 'Mrs. Sinkins' and *Alchemilla mollis* spill out onto the the path.**

Many plants that thrive in Mediterranean regions are particularly invaluable in dry, sunny gardens.

There are many areas that suffer increasingly droughtlike conditions, especially during the summer months, and many more that have low rainfall and fast-draining sandy or chalky soil. In addition to these naturally occurring dry regions, there are dry areas within most gardens. The ground at the foot of a house wall, for example, will receive less rain—the gutters carry away the precious liquid and quite often dispose of it in a manner wasteful to the gardener—and, to compound the problem, the foundation of the walls reduces the area where roots can seek moisture so there is more competition for the available damp. However, the good news for gardeners is that there is a large number of drought-tolerant perennials that will flourish in such dry and arid conditions.

Many plants that thrive in Mediterranean regions are particularly invaluable in dry, sunny gardens. Their silvery-gray foliage is attractive and provides a soothing backdrop to colorful flowers. *Anthemis punctata* subsp. *cupaniana* has finely cut gray foliage, and is covered with white daisies throughout June and July. It is a fast grower and will make a good-sized mound within only one or two seasons in dry conditions. Another species with pretty gray foliage is the *Dianthus* family, the pinks. They will thrive in a hot, dry bed, too, although they have to be replaced fairly frequently to prevent them from getting leggy. Actually, it is very easy, because pieces broken off and pushed in the ground in late summer will usually root, eliminating the need for seed trays and greenhouses. *Dianthus* cultivars all have distinctive gray foliage, are evergreen, and, although not splashy, the showy, clove-scented flowers have great charm. A famous old white variety, 'Mrs. Sinkins', which has fringed double flowers, has been overtaken by the superior 'White Ladies', which is shaggy with a pale green center, but both are sweetly scented. Of the old varieties, and it is well worth tracking these down, 'Inchmery' is very pale lavender-pink, and 'Sops-in-wine' has deep maroon flowers with uneven white markings on each petal. 'Brympton Red', which is taller than most, has single flowers with crimson petals marbled in deep rose. And this is only a tiny number of this enormous genus—there are many more of these beautiful old-fashioned flowers, and most of them will flourish in dry spots.

Another plant with handsome gray-green foliage is *Cerastium tomentosum*, which is often seen in old-fashioned gardens and is more commonly known as "snow-in-summer" due to its abundant clear white flowers. It is easy to grow and romps everywhere, but is never a problem, being easy to pull out. *Ballota pseudodictamnus* also has grayish-green downy foliage, with the added attraction of curious little balls of gray flowers along the white wooly stems in summer. It is evergreen, always rather a boon where herbaceous perennials are concerned.

particularly well when incorporated into "hot" color schemes, where the silvery foliage adds a cooling touch. In a larger bed, *Crambe*, a member of the cabbage family, makes a striking and dramatic addition, with large blue-gray cabbagelike leaves and an enormous hazy mass of tiny white flowers that run riot in summer. *Crambe maritima* is the one to look for. Its roots, if peeled and eaten, have the flavor of a mild radish and the crunchy consistency of a water chestnut.

With its dainty sprays of blooms, the spreading *Dicentra*, commonly known as Bear's breeches or Dutchman's trousers, is a delicate-looking but robust subject for a cool, dry bed. *D.* 'Stuart Boothman' carries finely cut slate-blue foliage with dangling, deep pink, heart-shaped flowers.

The spiky sword-shaped leaves of irises remain an attractive feature even when the plant is not in flower. *Iris pallida* is a tall bearded iris with a sheaf of narrow, blue-green leaves and lavender-blue flowers that appear in early summer. *I. pallida* retains its swordlike leaves all summer long and combines particularly well with a clump of *Salvia argentea*, which teams white flower spikes with a mass of enormous wooly silver-gray leaves. Other irises that will survive in dry and inhospitable sites include the attractive *Iris unguicularis*, which can be grown against a south-facing house wall, with stones and gravel around it. The blooms range in color from palest lavender to deepest violet, and appear both in early spring and, in mild weather, again in the late fall. They can be followed with the petite and fragrant *Iris reticulata*, which carries deeper violet flowers splashed with an orange-yellow central crest.

Crambe, makes a striking and dramatic addition.

Achillea, the yarrow of the wild, has a variety or two with finely cut, soft gray leaves. Its tiny flowers are clustered into flat-topped platelike flowerheads set on tall stalky stems. 'Moonshine' and 'Limelight' have primrose and lime-yellow flowers respectively, a pretty color combination that works

Left above: *Crambe maritima*, or seakale, offers a winning combination of clouds of white flowers and handsome blue-green, glaucous foliage. Thriving in coastal gardens, it is often grown as a vegetable for its edible stems.

Left below: **The dangling hearts of** *Dicentra spectablils* **enliven the garden between spring and summer.**

Right: **It is the stunning foliage rather than the flowers that distinguish** *Iris pallida* 'Aurea Variegata', **here seen thrusting up through a spring carpet of pink** *Anemone blanda*.

Above: *Iris unguicularis*, **native to the Mediterranean, needs a spot in the hottest, driest part of the garden. The cultivar shown here, 'Mary Barnard', appears in early spring and is a good plant for cutting for the house.**

Another plant that demands a dry situation is *Sisyrinchium striatum*, which has gray-green irislike leaves and produces short spikes of soft yellow flowers in midsummer. If you want a smaller-leafed wooly textured plant, chose *Stachys byzantina*, which has delightfully furry thick gray leaves with a silvery sheen. I prefer to prune its rather dull, magenta flowers; they tend to weaken the growth of the leaves if allowed to flourish.

Moving away from gray-foliaged sun-lovers, a plant that loves to be baked all summer long and requires no feeding, is the *Nerine*. This bulbous perennial comes from South Africa, which is why it will tolerate such inhospitably dry conditions. *Nerine bowdenii* has strap-shaped green leaves for most of the season and sends up graceful stems 24 in (60 cm) in height, topped with exotic pink flowers like a starry lily. It bursts into bloom in late summer, a time of year when color is scarce.

The perennial geraniums, of which there are a great many, are accommodating plants, thriving in many different conditions, and are happy to grow in a hot, dry border. Most of them have attractive flowers in colors ranging from mauvy blues through to pale pinks and white. The added bonus is that they will cover a lot of ground without being invasive or becoming a nuisance. The earliest to flower is the semi-evergreen *Geranium macrorrhizum*, which has the additional bonus of splendid

This bulbous perennial from South Africa will tolerate inhospitably dry conditions.

autumn colors in the pretty scalloped leaves. *G. maculatum*, which originates from North America, is a wonderful blush-lilac shade. In addition, it flowers for weeks in late spring, springing up to about 24 in (60 cm). *G. endressii*, of which there are several named varieties, flowers constantly during the summer, with a generous show of delicate pale pink blooms.

The dry ground found at the base of a high wall in full sun need not be barren. If there is not even enough room for a narrow border, grow a clematis in a container. You can take your pick of the pinks, mauves, purples, reds, some yellows, blues, and of course white, so there ought to be one that will suit the material of the walls behind it. Clematis also flower all the way through the season, starting with the well-known *Clematis montana* group, which flower in early summer. *C. montana* itself is white, *C. m.* 'Elizabeth' an exquisite soft pink, and *C. m.* var. *rubens* a powdery purple-pink. They are rampant growers, so it is best to attach a framework of support wires to the wall before planting the clematis, which will make the job of tying in much easier when the plant is growing. A light clear-up after flowering is all these clematis require, and there is the added advantage that *Clematis montana* types are content on walls facing in any

direction. Flowering even earlier, the attractive evergreen *Clematis armandii* carries vanilla-scented flowers in early to mid-spring. These creamy white sprays look startling against the long, dark, ribbed leaves. This is a slightly tender plant and will need a south- or west-facing wall, with some shelter from the wind. However, it is well worth the trouble taken.

From the many large-flowered, summer-flowering clematis, choose *C.* 'Duchess of Edinburgh', which has double white blooms with lime-green outer sepals; *C.* 'Beauty of Worcester', with its large deep-blue flowers; or *C.* 'Marie Boisselot', which

Far left: **Because it self-seeds prodigiously, *Sisyrinchium striatum* needs a few square feet of sunny space to do itself justice.**

Left: ***Nerine bowdenii* should be planted close to the surface, and, ideally, up against the base of a south-** **facing wall where the bulbs can ripen and thus produce a mass of pink lilylike flowers in early fall.**

Right: ***Clematis montana* 'Freda' is less vigorous than other plants in the group, making it suitable for a smaller garden.**

Helenium will contribute a drift of bold color to any bed.

carries pure white flowers continuously from mid-spring to early autumn. In spring, *C. macropetala* has a multitude of little, hairy, nodding blue bells, and in late summer any of the *C. viticella* is worth growing, especially the beautiful 'Mme. Julia Correvon', which is a luscious wine red with golden stamens. Also worth considering is the more unusual *C. rehderiana*, which is heavily scented and covered in tiny soft-yellow flowers.

If you have a fairly wide bed set against a house wall, it can be treated as a proper flower border and planted thickly with sun-loving plants. The material of the house will be the background to your planting, so if the wall is of red brick, heat it up even more with a planting of yellow, bronze, and a dash of cool white. Perhaps include that staple of the sunny late-summer border, *Helenium*. Its large daisy-shaped flowers are available in a range of rich, velvety bronzes, oranges, and golds, and will contribute a drift of bold color to any flowerbed. Mass it with the profuse white blooms of *Anaphalis*, and the tall *Macleaya*, known as the plume poppy because of its immense grayish poppy-plant leaves and feathery plumes of pinky-beige flowers. The roots of *Macleaya* will run as far underground as it is tall above and it does need to be kept in check. Daylilies also associate very well with heleniums. Try some of the darker-colored varieties, such as *Hemerocallis* 'Golden Chimes' which is a rich yellow with brown on the reverse. Alternatively, *H.* 'Alan' is a striking mahogany shade, while *H.* 'Stafford' has scarlet flowers with green-yellow throats.

By far the most difficult place to grow things is in dry shade beneath trees, particularly if it is run through with roots, twigs, and other dusty debris. Plants that will thrive in these conditions are discussed in Shady spots (*see pages* 24–35).

Right: **Heleniums such as this one, *H.* 'Moerheim Beauty', bring warm, bright tones to** **the late-summer border. They look best when massed with plants of creamy coloring.**

DRY SITES GALLERY

Achillea 'Lachsschönheit'

Height: 24–30 in (60–75 cm), spread: 18–24 in (45–60 cm); flowers in summer; fully hardy

This form of the common yarrow has flat heads composed of many tiny flowerets which vary slightly in coloring, the overall effect being a soft pink brick color, which is seen at its best when situated next to plants with purple foliage, such as *Berberis thunbergii* f. *atropurpurea*.

Crambe cordifolia

Height: 8 ft (2.5 m), spread: 5 ft (1.5 m); flowers in mid- to late summer; fully hardy

Clouds of small white flowers give this plant a misty effect not unlike *Gypsophila*. Plant at the front of a border, where the large, gray-green leaves, ruffled at the edges, can spill out onto a path or terrace.

Geranium sanguineum 'Album'

Height: 12 in (30 cm), spread: 16 in (40 cm); flowers in summer; fully hardy

This is a low, spreading geranium for the front of a border. The clear, fresh green leaves make neats clumps, above which emerge the pure white flowers. The plant does not spoil in wet weather.

Linaria purpurea

Height: 3 ft (90 cm), spread: 2 ft (60 cm); flowers in midsummer to early autumn; fully hardy

Wiry stems clothed in short, thin leaves carry spires of purple flowers, which also appear on side shoots. Plants do well in a sunny bed or rock garden, and they will self-seed freely between cracks in a pavement.

Mentha suaveolens 'Variegata' (Apple mint)

Height: 18 in (45 cm), spread: indefinite; flowers in summer; fully hardy

The pretty cream variegation of the soft wooly leaves makes this mint, with its fruity fragrance, a good choice for a dry garden.

Perovskia 'Blue Spire'

Height: 4 ft (1.2 m), spread: 3 ft (90 cm); flowers in late summer; fully hardy

Lavender spires above silver-gray leaves bring welcome color to the late-summer border. Technically speaking, this is a shrub, but to encourage good shoots and plenty of flowers, it is best to cut it down each year to ground level.

Romneya coulteri

Height: 8 ft (2.5 m), spread: 6½ ft (2 m); flowers in midsummer to early autumn; half hardy

Native to California, these showy flowers, with large, poppy heads offset by attractive blue-gray foliage, make an exotic splash in the garden. The crumpled, white, papery petals unfold around prominent, bright yellow stamens.

Salvia officinalis (Sage)

Height 2 ft (60 cm), spread: 3 ft (90 cm); flowers in summer; fully hardy

Commonly available as the gray-leafed, violet-flowered type, and also *Salvia purpurea*, the purple-leafed sage, and *Salvia officinalis* 'Icterina', which has leaves variegated with lime-green and yellow but no, or very few, flowers.

Scabiosa caucasica

Height and spread: 2 ft (60 cm); flowers in early summer to early autumn; fully hardy

The blues, lilacs, mauves, and creamy whites of the scabious, or pincushion flower, are invaluable in a dry, sunny border. They prefer a slightly limy soil, so a position under a wall is ideal. *Scabiosa caucasica* carries pale blue blooms over a long season. It needs regular division in spring to ensure good flowering.

Sisyrinchium striatum 'Aunt May'

Height: 3 ft (90 cm), spread: 10 in (25 cm); flowers in early to midsummer; fully hardy

The *Sisyrinchium* mentioned in the text is a very easy plant and seeds itself prolifically. One or two plants soon turn into a large clump, and seedlings will appear dotted about the garden quite some distance from the original. *S. s.* 'Aunt May' doesn't seed itself, however, and has the advantage, in addition to the pretty, straw-yellow flowers, of being variegated, the narrow swordlike leaves striped creamy yellow.

Top left: **Linaria purpurea**

Top center: **Perovskia 'Blue Spire'**

Top right: **Salvia officinalis**

Above left: **Geranium sanguineum 'Album'**

Above center: **Romneya coulteri**

Above right: **Achillea 'Lachsschönheit'**

Far left: **Mentha suaveolens 'Variegata'**

Left: **Crambe cordifolia**

Opposite page: **Dicentra eximia 'Snowdrift'**

A carpet of ground-covering perennials will help to suppress weeds and mask an expanse of bare soil. Introducing plants that spread quickly will make a garden look more mature than it actually is, and rampant growers can even be used as an exciting alternative to grass.

GROUND COVER

All herbaceous perennials are, in effect, ground covering. But the term, as used here, refers to any plant that forms a thick mat of leaves with an extensive network of roots, which will hide soil from view and prevent weeds from getting a toehold in the soil. Ground-cover plants can be grown under existing taller plantings, of both trees and shrubs. This is useful in areas where it might be hard to get another, larger item to flourish, or where the shrubs are not large enough to allow taller underplantings, but are big enough to allow the earth beneath them to be visible, a visibility that can let in weeds.

Ground cover can also be used as an alternative to grass, flowing over gravel or stone, softening hard edges, and reducing the necessity for mowing or too much spraying. If you are considering using ground cover as an alternative lawn, it is important to realize that anything other than grass will never give so fine, so smooth, so even an effect. To talk of replacing grass with other plants means accepting a green area that will, whatever you do, be a bit uneven to look at, a bit bumpy to walk on, and will require patience to establish. It will not be a lawn. Do not, however, despite these restrictions, be deterred from the attempt, and if the weekly demands of lawn mowing cannot be met, the ground-cover alternative is worth the initial effort.

Evergreen ground cover is useful in areas where the ground is always visible but is, for one reason or another, not suitable to be used as a mixed border. An island bed in the center of a driveway, for example, which might contain a single tree or a small group of trees, could be planted with one of the most useful of all ground-cover plants, *Vinca*, commonly known as periwinkle. The most common forms of *Vinca* are *Vinca major* and *Vinca*

Above: **In winter, when the colors of summer have passed, the variegated ivy will be the predominant feature of this island bed, consorting well with the rough stone.**

Below: **The periwinkle, *Vinca major* 'Variegata', is a true carpeter. Having colorful flowers and foliage, being disease-free, and possessing a willingness to thrive in shade are its other virtues.**

Vinca is one of the most useful of all ground cover plants.

minor, a simple nomenclature that differentiates between the size of leaf and the flower, although the plants themselves are not very different. *V. major* 'Variegata' has leaves splashed and edged with cream, and rich violet-blue flowers. It is a rampant grower, rooting wherever the shoots touch the ground, and can be kept in check with an annual trim with the shears in winter. It appears to be impervious to the cold and will grow just as

exuberantly facing due north and with some overhead shade as it will when given plenty of light. *V. minor* has more varied forms, some with flowers in white, purple, or violet blue.

Equally vigorous and versatile is *Ajuga reptans*, commonly known as bugle. *Ajuga reptans* 'Atropurpurea' is perhaps the most attractive variety, its glossy dark purple leaves tinged with bronze. It will swiftly make itself at home in almost any situation,

Above: **The creeping *Ajuga reptans* 'Atropurpurea', at the base of a multistemmed ornamental cherry tree, spreads freely and makes a thick, weedproof mat. It thrives in sun and shade.**

Left: **The wood spurge,**
***Euphorbia amygdaloides* var.**
***robbiae*, roots itself freely**
and, given a shady position
and plenty of space, makes
an outstanding evergreen
ground-cover plant.

Above left and right: **Given a position out of the wind,** ***Euphorbia characias* is a noble plant, its huge acid green bracts studded with black eyes. The plant grows to a height of about 5 ft (1.5 m).** ***Euphorbia characias* subsp.** ***wulfenii*, here complemented by a planting of origano and golden marjoram, is even taller than the species, growing to about 6½ ft (2 m). The bracts do not have black eyes.**

not being averse to shade, drought, or even soil occupied by the roots of something else. In fact, it is quite a bully and will ruthlessly smother smaller plants, so take care and either give it plenty of room, or restrict its growth with a barrier of hard edging.

Less vigorous, but equally dense, is *Pachysandra terminalis*, a much undervalued perennial. There are two varieties; one with smooth, glossy green leaves and a variegated form patterned with creamy white. There is a flower, of a sort, but it is the little round-ended and toothed leaves, forming neat rosettes on each stem, that give the plant its charm. *Pachysandra* gives no trouble—it will happily occupy the space allotted to it in a very few seasons, although the variegated form is slower off the mark than the plain green variety.

Taller, and more invasive again, is *Euphorbia amygdaloides* var. *robbiae*. In early spring, this plant exudes an

aura of freshness, with its rich, green, perfect leaves and intensely yellowish-green bracts. Although an evergreen, many new stems are pushed up annually, and as long as you cut out the old ones on a mild early winter morning, the fresh appearance is not impaired by the association with old growth. The trimming is purely for esthetic purposes—the plants do not need it to improve their ability to grow.

There are other useful euphorbias, some a little smaller, one or two enormous, that can also be used as ground cover. The low-growing, blue-gray *Euphorbia myrsinites* will send out stems 12 in (30 cm) long during the summer, which, in the following spring, will carry yellowish-green bracts. This is a well-behaved plant, so perhaps strictly speaking it is not ground cover, but it thrives in sunny, dry positions and will do very well at the base of a lanky tree or pushed into crevices on a brick or stone terrace.

Ivies (*Hedera*) are, technically speaking, herbaceous perennials and can be most effective ground-cover plants, although they are more commonly seen clambering up tree trunks, fences, and walls. If you wish to grow ivy as ground cover, it is important to make sure that, where it meets the vertical, it is prevented from ascending. Ivies will grow well in shade, so you can plant them to make a continuous carpet beneath hedges, and around the base of trees. There is an enormous number of varieties available, so the selection is personal, although on the whole the smaller-leafed types tend to look best at ground level, as the debris and the rain wash through them, whereas the bigger leaves can become ragged, brown, and limp, like crumpled brown paper scattered on the ground.

Alchemilla mollis, lady's mantle, will provide attractive ground cover. The velvety green leaves, covered in soft down, trap glistening, jewellike drops of water after the rain. A mass of acid-green flowers rises above the leaves in spring. *A. mollis* is a prolific self-seeder, and as a result, its use as ground cover is preferable to a position in a mixed border, where seedlings will require constant removal. Accordingly, an isolated position suits it perfectly; an island bed in a driveway, for example. *Alchemilla*

Alchemilla mollis will provide attractive ground cover. The velvety green leaves, covered in soft down, trap glistening, jewellike drops of water after the rain.

The largest of the euphorbias, *Euphorbia characias*, would not normally be considered as ground cover, but if you have room, it is exciting to use it this way. Tolerant of shade and heavily self-seeding, in dry conditions it will soon form a great dome of huge heads, dense with lime-green bracts, each with a single black eye. It has narrow gray-green leaves.

Right: *Alchemilla mollis* **is a ground-cover plant** *par excellence*, **clumps of which will appear all over the place once a plant has been established in the garden.**

Your "lawn" will be composed of three different greens, creating a tapestrylike effect.

flowers of *Stachys byzantina* are not particularly attractive; the felty quality so handsome in the leaves tends to look rather moldy on the flowers, so it is worth removing them as soon as they appear. Flowering also tends to weaken the leaves, making the whole plant look like an old dishcloth.

A most striking plant for sunny ground cover, and not particular as to soil, is *Persicaria affinis* 'Donald Lowndes'. This flowers in late summer, putting forward a myriad of stiff little brushes of pink spikes, above strap-shaped, apple green leaves with bronze stripes, an altogether eye-catching sight. The flowering period runs into autumn; and during the winter months

alpina is a smaller and better-behaved plant, with an old-fashioned Victorian charm. The backs of the leaves are silvery and silky, and will stay that way even when dried and pressed between the pages of a book.

There are some curiosities that can be used as ground cover, including a splendidly sinister plant called *Ophiopogon planiscapus* 'Nigrescens'. This is sometimes known as "black grass," which is what it resembles, but in fact it is not a grass at all, but an evergreen member of the lily family It increases slowly, so plant a few clumps at a time. In early fall, it produces poisonous-looking berries: small, shiny, mauve-blue spheres carried on wiry stems. It is supposed to benefit from sun, but grows well enough in shade to be a useful ground-cover plant.

The soft, felty, gray leaves of *Stachys byzantina*, evocatively known as lamb's ears, also provide excellent ground cover. *Stachys* and *Ophiopogon* make a striking combination and work well together because, although contrasting, there is an affinity between them in tone rather than hue. The ruddy mauve

Above: **In a hundred years' time, the space taken up by the black leaves of *Ophiopogon planiscapus* 'Nigrescens' will be completely covered over by the Irish yew in the center.**

Right: **Different thymes have been planted on a bank, covering what could be an awkward space to maintain and making a pleasing foil to the penstemons planted in the bed opposite.**

the leaves remain a tangled, light, gingery brown, not unlike the color of winter beech leaves. Offering decorative foliage and early spring flowers, *Bergenia*, a large-leafed evergreen, is another excellent choice for ground cover, especially in shaded spots. There are several good varieties, most with pink-mauve flowers held rather low among the leaves on sturdy stems, but also some white-flowering ones, of which 'Silberlicht' and 'Bressingham White' are among the best. 'Bressingham White' has small leaves, less prone to the tattiness induced by winter winds. Some varieties have large leaves that turn attractive shades of rich purple or red in the fall and winter.

When it comes to using a ground-cover perennial as an alternative to grass, the usual choice for this purpose is a camomile lawn. However, the effort of keeping the weeds out, both early in your lawn-making and as the plants eventually join together, is enormous. An easier and quicker choice might be a thyme lawn, into which the yellow and the variegated forms can be mixed, bearing in mind that they are weaker and smaller than the regular green thyme. Your "lawn" will be composed of three different greens, creating a tapestrylike effect. Adding a handful of what is sold nowadays as "meadow seeds" will introduce an extra element of colorful wildflowers into your herb lawn.

Below: **A very wide bed can be edged with ground-cover plants such as *Stachys byzantina*, so that the taller perennials and shrubs can be accentuated by the low carpet at their feet.**

GROUND COVER GALLERY

Ajuga reptans (Common bugle)

Height: 6 in (15 cm), spread: 2–3 ft (60–90 cm); flowers in spring and early summer; fully hardy

Short spikes of blue flowers peep above the glossy leaves of this creeping, mat-forming perennial. A. r. 'Atropurpurea' has bronze-tinted purple foliage.

Arabis alpina subsp. caucasica 'Variegata'

Height: 10 in (25 cm), spread: 2 ft (60 cm); flowers in late spring; fully hardy

This rockcress forms low mats which spread rapidly. The cut edges of the cream and green leaves are very distinctive, and make a most striking ground cover for a good-sized area. The small four-petaled flowers are creamy white, and as all the petals fall, spiky little stems are left above the leaves.

Arenaria balearica

Height: 1¼ in (3 cm), spread: 20 in (50 cm); flowers in late spring to summer; fully hardy

Masses of tiny, white, star-shaped flowers, each on its own stem, appear above the dense, mosslike mats of bright green, foliage. This small prostrate perennial is evergreen except in very severe winters, and will grow in a damp soil, including one that is stony, as well as coping with drier conditions. It thrives in a shady spot.

Bergenia 'Rosi Klose' (Elephant's ears)

Height: 12 in (30 cm), spread: 12 in (30 cm); flowers in mid- to late spring; fully hardy

Bergenias provide dense ground cover and are tolerant of a wide range of conditions. B. 'Rosi Klose' carries charming salmon-pink flowers and spoon-shaped leaves. B. 'Silverlicht' and B. 'Bressingham White' both carry white flowers.

Epimedium (Barrenwort, bishop's miter)

Height: 8–16 in (20–40 cm); spread: 12–24 in (30–60 cm); flowers in spring; hardy

There is quite a choice here, and almost any that are available are worth having. The dainty flowers range from red to white to yellow, but cut the leaves down in late winter to encourage the flowers to be seen later. The heart-shaped, horizontally held leaves, with red and brown markings, are pretty in their own right. Epimediums do best in shade. The copper-tinged young leaves of E. grandiflorum 'Rose Queen' contrast well with the deep rose-pink flowers with long white spurs. E. × perralchicum has large yellow flowers.

Gypsophila repens 'Dubia'

Height: 4 in (10 cm), spread: 12 in (30 cm); flowers in summer; fully hardy

This semi-evergreen, mat-forming, prostrate plant bears horizontally held heads of pale pink flowers. It has slightly fleshy, gray-green, lance-shaped leaves with pink tinges.

Hedera helix 'Kolibri'

Height: 3 ft (90 cm), spread: 10 ft (3 m); frost hardy

The common ivy, H. helix, is widely used for ground cover. H. h. 'Kolibri' has small, five-lobed, mid-green leaves that are splashed with white.

Origanum vulgare 'Aureum'

Height: 12 in (30 cm), spread: 3 ft (90 cm); flowers in mid spring and early summer; fully hardy

Marjoram seeds itself everywhere, and this yellow-leafed form is no exception. The aromatic leaves, which become greener in late summer, form a low, spreading mound. This is ideal for ground-cover as no weeds will grow up through it.

Stachys byzantina (Lamb's ears)

Height: 16 in (40 cm), spread: 20 in (50 cm); flowers in summer; fully hardy

The wooly, gray-green leaves create a handsome carpet. They do best in a sunny position in well-drained soil. S. b. 'Cotton Boll' has spikes of silver-white bobbles.

Vinca major

Height: 14 in (35 cm), spread: 14 in (35 cm); flowers in mid spring and early summer; fully hardy

The carpets of foliage are studded with bright blue flowers. Periwinkles do well in shady spots, making them an ideal choice for growing under trees or shrubs.

Use foliage to bring interesting shapes, textures, and color into the garden for part or even all of the year and to provide a stunning foil for other plants. Many perennials combine exciting foliage with attractive flowers; others offer leaves that are worthy of a place in their own right.

FOLIAGE

Left: **For a visually exciting scheme without a flower in sight, combine foliage plants with different-shaped leaves. Here grasses and hostas, buddleia, and *Lonicera pileata* join forces to make a lush planting below a multi-stemmed ornamental tree.**

Above: ***Helleborus foetidus* is a native of Great Britain, its curious, green, cup-shaped flowers enlivening the evergreen foliage in the winter months.**

Right: ***Helleborus argutifolius* still carries its flowers in abundance in spring, here accompanying the new leaves of *Alchemilla mollis* and rheum and the flowers of bluebells and tulips.**

Evergreen plants provide interest in the winter garden, and the emergent leaves of new growth are positively exciting in early spring.

Perennials with attractive foliage are invaluable for several reasons. First, foliage lasts longer than flowers, providing a decorative focus in the garden for many months, or, in the case of evergreens, all year round. Second, many perennials have foliage that is decorative in its own right, offering qualities such as striking seasonal color effects, pleasing textures, or leaf shapes that provide beautiful contrasts to other plants. And third, foliage can act as a wonderful foil to colorful flowers.

In winter, and during the early part of the year, foliage plays an especially important part in the planning of the garden. Evergreen plants provide interest in the winter garden, and the emergent leaves of new growth are positively exciting in early spring. The hellebores are extremely valuable additions to the winter garden, particularly *Helleborus foetidus*, with its sharply divided leaves and green, nodding, bell-like flowers, often tipped with a dull crimson, which flower from January on. *Helleborus niger*, the Christmas rose, is another beautiful thing, with waxy white flowers, sometimes stained pink, and large yellow stamens. The toothed leaves are glossy green when new, darker when older—a pleasing and subtle contrast.

The bold, leathery leaves of the bergenias hang on throughout the winter, but they do not always look quite as handsome as one might wish. Because the leaves are large and their stems rather long, they are often buffeted by winter winds and develop a torn and ragged look, with dried-up or soggy browning leaves still firmly attached to the stems and flapping about in the wind. To prevent this sorry sight, give your bergenias an autumn clean-up—trim the dead or decaying leaves and snip off any really large or loose foliage.

Cyclamen hederifolium, the autumn-flowering cyclamen, retains its perfect marbled leaves throughout winter and well into spring. With a dark green background and remarkably patterned in silver gray, these leaves bear close inspection. Each one is different, varying both in size and pattern. Once established, the plant spreads quickly, and a clump planted under a deciduous shrub or tree, or even beneath an evergreen tree, will soon enliven a piece of ground that would otherwise be bare and neglected. Take care, however, to leave the corms undisturbed in

Below: **Resembling the design for a stained-glass window, the leaves of *Iris pallida* 'Aurea Variegata', which grow to 2 ft (60 cm) long, make a perfect fan, glowing with the sun shining through them.**

Right: **Simple foliage plantings are often the most telling, as in this pairing of two variegated irises, *I. pallida* 'Aurea Variegata' and *I. pseudacorus* 'Variegata'.**

Far right: **The exoticism of the emerging leaves of *Paeonia mlokosewitschii* is prolonged by the appearance of the lemon-yellow flowers.**

summer. At this time of year, the leaves disappear, and curious spherical seed heads attached to coiled springs appear. It is easy to overlook these earth-colored seed heads and casually push the hoe or hand-fork across an apparently empty space, destroying the seed heads in the process and inadvertently impeding the enlarging of the group.

By late winter and into early spring, the garden is on the move. Assuming that the weather is not too unkind, lots of growth starts to appear. One of the most exotic and exciting appearances is that of the peony. From the first showing of the tips to the time when the leaves and stems are some 18 in (45 cm) high, the showy foliage is a glossy brownish-red, and makes an excellent foil for the fresh, apple-green new leaves of primulas. Carefully chosen primula flowers can also look perfect against a background of peony leaves. For a strong contrast, choose the double white form of the common primrose, *Primula vulgaris*. Equally effective is the common primula itself, the soft yellow, apple green, and matte textures of the flower and leaves contrasting well with the shiny, shoe-leather tones of the peony leaves. Later, as the primroses die down and the peonies expand, the former's now flowerless leaves are covered by the more interesting leaves of the latter. Many peonies also have rich autumn colors in their leaves, so there are compensations for the short flowering season of this genus.

Also emerging early in the year, and in some cases flowering, too, are the irises. Most iris foliage is gray-green and narrow, and persists even after flowering, but *Iris pallida* var. *dalmatica* has grayish leaves with a steely blue tinge, and the foliage retains its color all through summer and into the fall. *Iris pallida* subsp. *pallida* 'Variegata' has pale gray-green leaves striped with golden yellow. The lavender-blue flowers of these irises also have the added bonus of scent. Another iris with variegated leaves is *Iris pseudacorus* 'Variegata', which has yellow and ivory stripes in springtime, fading to a fresh green by

Most iris foliage is gray-green and narrow, and persists even after flowering.

the summer months. With foliage very similar to the iris, the variegated *Sisyrinchium striatum* 'Aunt May' has sword-shaped leaves marked with creamy white stripes. Its clustered flowers are a pretty primrose yellow, but it is the flat, narrow evergreen leaves that really set this plant apart.

For a wide choice of striking variegation, wonderful color and varying leaf size, hostas are hard to beat. They are best grown in light shade, although they are not so intolerant of dry conditions as might be supposed. The small-leafed *Hosta* 'Albomarginata' (*fortunei*) is just that, with narrow, dull green, white-edged leaves. *Hosta undulata* var. *albomarginata* has larger leaves that are rich green in color and have a broad white margin. For beautiful, large, ribbed leaves in a wonderful blue-green, *Hosta sieboldiana* var. *elegans* is one of the very best varieties, and there are ever more and more named hostas being

produced with this silvery blue-green coloring. Yellow-leafed hostas tend to become green as the summer advances, but *Hosta fortunei* f. *aurea* looks incredibly fresh—almost artificial, in fact, when seen in the half-light of a wet spring day.

Come midsummer, many excellent foliage plants are adding flowers to their charms. The old cottage favorite, *Cerastium tomentosum*, commonly known as snow-in-summer, has an abundance of clear white flowers, and as the plant spreads itself around at ground level, the name is apt. When not in flower, its little silvery gray, felted leaves smother the ground, meandering charmingly over banks and stones.

Some notably large and dramatic leaves are to be found among the evergreen *Phormium*, or New Zealand flax. These are not typical of the growth of herbaceous perennials in general and are often classed as shrubs, although in colder climates they will be cut down by severe winters. The enormous spiky leaves of the *Phormium* can grow to as much as 10 ft (3 m) in height, although it takes many years before the plants get so large. There are some curiously colored and striped varieties; the well-known *Phormium tenax* has sharply pointed leathery gray-green leaves and *Phormium tenax* Purpureum Group has leaves with bronze and coppery tones. Both are hard to beat for sheer exoticism. If you live in a cold climate, don't expect flowers; phormiums only flower in warm climates, but with such dramatic sword-shaped leaves, who needs flowers? The black tufts of *Ophiopogon planiscapus* 'Nigrescens', with elegant, strap-like leaves echoing the larger phormium in shape, will soon spread to make a most satisfying clump. The plant is a curiosity, best positioned where

Right above: In a few years, this border, newly planted with *Hosta sieboldiana* var. *elegans*, will be a truly splendid sight, as the immense glaucous leaves, topped by spires of pale, silvery lavender spires, smother the ground.

Right below: *Hosta* 'Antioch', with its wide leaves with broad, creamy margins, will shortly be eclipsed by the campanulas and lilies, but at this stage in the season it is still holding its own.

Far right: Another hosta, this time the yellow-margined *H. fortunei* var. *aureomarginata*, looks wonderful planted under the golden-leaved elders and *Philadelphus*.

the unusual black leaves will afford some contrast. A path bordered with *Ophiopogon*, for example, with the thin black leaves growing half across stone or gravel would act as a perfect foil for this exotic-looking perennial.

An unusual and elegant clematis with feature foliage is the herbaceous *Clematis recta* 'Purpurea', a plant that will climb to 4 ft (1.2 m) high if given support, or can be grown to tumble down a bank or over a low wall. The leaves are an unusual purplish-blue, and the flowers are small and creamy but short-lived.

From the sublime to the ridiculous, at least in terms of size, is *Macleaya cordata*; the vast stems grow to 7 ft (2.2 m) and carry beautiful, multi-lobed, sage-green leaves with serrated edges and a contrasting gray-white underside. The flowers, although large, are delicate and lacy rather than bold or showy.

Below: **For a dramatic statement, *Phormium tenax* is hard to beat. It throws out huge flower stems up to 10 ft (3 m) high, followed by a myriad of shiny reddish-brown seed pods.**

Phormiums only flower in warm climates, but with such dramatic sword-shaped leaves, who needs flowers?

FOLIAGE GALLERY

Dierama pulcherrimum

Height: 5 ft (1.5 m), spread: 2 ft (60 cm); flowers in summer; frost hardy

The wandflower is a curious plant with long, narrow leaves. Tall, wiry stems support pendulous heads of pinky mauve, bell-shaped flowers. It is something to grow near the house where its shape can be best appreciated. Plant in a sheltered spot.

Helleborus argutifolius

Height: 2½ ft (75 cm), spread: 2½ ft (75 cm); flowers in late winter and early spring; frost hardy

The sage-green leaves of this evergreen hellebore are made up of three spiny-toothed leaflets. The gray veining creates a marbled effect. Cup-shaped, apple-green flowers are carried on thick, canelike stems.

Heuchera micrantha var. diversifolia 'Palace Purple'

Height: 18 in (45 cm), spread: 18 in (45 cm); flowers in early and midsummer; hardy

The bronze-purple leaves, growing to about 4 in (10 cm) long and with a slight metallic sheen, form little hummocks. The sprays of creamy white flowers borne on dark stems contrast well with the foliage.

Hosta 'Frances Williams'

Height: 2 ft (60 cm), spread: 3 ft (90 cm); flowers in early summer; fully hardy

Deep blue-green, heart-shaped leaves with green-yellow margins and sprays of grayish-white flowers grace this hosta, which does best in full shade.

Hosta 'Golden Tiara'

Height: 12 in (30 cm), spread: 20 in (50 cm); flowers in summer; fully hardy

This is a vigorous but compact hosta bearing mid-green leaves with yellow margins and deep lavender flowers striped with purple.

Iris pallida subsp. pallida

Height: 3–4 ft (90–120 cm), spread: 12–18 in (30–45 cm); flowers in late spring and early summer; fully hardy

Bearded irises are prized for their flowers, but they also offer handsome sword-shaped leaves. *I. p.* subsp. *pallida* combines soft blue flowers and blue-green leaves. Six flowers are carried on each stem.

Lychnis coronaria (Dusty miller, rose campion)

Height: 2 ft (60 cm), spread: 18 in (45 cm); flowers in summer; fully hardy

Gray multibranched stems carry felted gray leaves and rich magenta flowers, which are attractive to butterflies. This prolific self-seeder thrives in a dry, sunny site.

Morina longifolia

Height: 3 ft (90 cm), spread: 12 in (30 cm); flowers in summer; fully hardy

Those who didn't know any better might think this a thistle and uproot it. The leaves are similar—long, mid-green, recurved, and spiny—but from these leaves, which are kept close to the ground in a rosette, arise tall green spires that open to white, often pink-tinged, flowers held by a green calyx. The plant likes a little moisture, but well-drained soil.

Paeonia mlokosewitschii

Height: 28 in (70 cm), spread: 28 in (70 cm); flowers in spring; fully hardy

This beautiful peony, also known as 'Molly the Witch', has bowl-shaped, lemon-yellow flowers. The soft bluish-green foliage maintains the interest once the flowers have passed. All peonies do best on a sunny site.

Phlomis russeliana

Height: 3 ft (90 cm), spread: 2 ft (60 cm); flowers in late spring to early autumn; fully hardy

The stems of this evergreen are interrupted at intervals by spheres of hooded yellow flowers. The mid-green leaves are heart-shaped and rather coarse. It is not fussy in its soil requirements and will stand some buffeting from the wind.

Phlox paniculata 'Norah Leigh'

Height: 3 ft (90 cm), spread: 3 ft (90 cm);

The attractive leaves, variegated in creamy yellow, and lilac flowers show up particularly well with something dark behind them. Keep the plant slightly damp at the foot.

Planting Holding the plant by the root ball, place it in the hole so it sits securely on the bottom. The plant will quickly become established if its roots can push through the soil easily.

Dividing Lift the plant with a fork, making sure not to damage the roots, and carefully shake off the loose soil. Divide the clump by hand, selecting pieces that have healthy roots and shoots.

Deadheading Remove spent flower heads with a pair of pruning shears. This encourages new flowers to develop and helps to strengthen the roots.

care and cultivation

Perennials are not particularly demanding in their requirements, and by following a few basic rules of care and cultivation you will be able to enjoy a garden that is full of healthy and thriving plants. Choosing perennials to suit the conditions in your garden is the easiest way to make sure of growing success, so refer to the previous chapters to find out which plants will thrive where.

Buying perennials

Perennials usually put on a good deal of growth in their first season, so, when buying new plants, don't be unduly concerned if they look small. The important thing is to choose a plant that is strong and healthy. A responsible and reputable nursery will have grown the plant from seed or from root cuttings. Garden centers usually buy their plants in from wholesalers, which makes it a little harder for the purchaser to be sure of the quality of the stock. There is a chance that the plant will have been forced in a plastic tunnel or greenhouse, and might have produced plenty of lush new growth that is actually weak. So don't be seduced by plants that look too full and leafy, particularly early in the season. Later on, from midsummer, a lot of perennials are making more leaf anyway.

Don't be afraid to knock the plant gently out of its pot to have a look at the roots. If you cannot see any, this may mean that the plant is either not growing or has been repotted recently. The latter is only likely to have taken place in a nursery, and the nurseryman will be able to tell you whether or not this is the case. If so, the plant is best left in its pot for two or three weeks to make sure that it is rooted through.

Planting perennials

Container-grown perennials can, in theory, be planted out at any time of the year. In cold areas, however, planting in spring gives the roots time to become established before the first winter. Avoid planting in waterlogged, frozen, or dry summer soil.

Remove any weeds or large stones and dig a hole that is big enough for the root ball of the plant. Depending on the soil, a sprinkling of organic matter will provide valuable nourishment. If the plants are very dry, immerse them in a bucket of water and hold them down until the bubbles cease to rise. Then let the pots drain so the soil is not dripping wet. With one hand firmly on the surface of the soil, invert the pot and remove the plant. Carefully tease the roots out a little, to break up the pot-shaped mass of potting medium and roots.

Place the plant in the prepared hole, making sure the top of the soil around the plant is on the same level as the ground. Supporting the stem with one hand, scoop the earth into place all around the plant. Press the soil down firmly to make sure the plant won't rock around in the wind or be easily uprooted by animals. Water the plant thoroughly and trim away any part of it that looks crisp or dead. It is advisable, even when you have selected a plant you like in full flower, to snip off the flowers; this helps the roots become well established.

Dividing perennials

Many perennials benefit from being divided every few years. This discourages them from forming too thick and matted a mass of roots and helps to freshen the plant so it will produce more flowers.

Division is carried out when the plant is dormant, usually during the winter months, but choose a month when the weather is good and the ground is neither waterlogged nor frozen. Lift the plant from the ground, making sure you do not damage the roots. Shake off loose soil and gently pull apart the clump of roots with your hands until it splits into two pieces. For larger clumps or thicker roots, you may have to use garden forks or a spade. Make sure the new clumps have plenty of young shoots and healthy roots. Finally, replant the divided clumps in the ground. Although a well-filled flowerbed is a splendid sight, leave a bit of room around plants, so they can increase themselves and also benefit from rain.

Routine care

Caring for your perennials is largely about common sense and observation. Tall plants, such as delphiniums, must be staked, since their hollow stems are inclined to snap in windy weather. Plants with lush leaves close to the ground, such as hostas, are a lure for slugs, so they must be protected with antislug material. Unless you need seed for propagation, deadhead regularly. Be prepared to weed, of course, and be vigilant against pests. But, above all, enjoy what you have planted and keep it all in good heart. As you become more familiar with what you grow, you will be able to assess a plant's particular needs and treat it accordingly.

Picture credits

The publishers would like to thank the photographers and garden owners for allowing them to reproduce the photographs on the following pages:

Endpapers: J. Harpur; 1 J. Harpur/RHS Wisley, Surrey; 2 J. Harpur/ Dolwen, Powys; 3 J. Harpur/RHS Wisley, Surrey; 4–5 J. Harpur/design: Xa Tollemache, Chelsea Flower Show 1997; 5 J. Harpur/Garden in the Woods, Framlingham, MA; 6 top J. Harpur; 6–7 top centre M. Harpur/Beth Chatto Gardens, Essex; 6 below J. Harpur; 7 top J. Harpur; 7 below M. Harpur/Beth Chatto Gardens, Essex; 8–9 J. Harpur/design: Bob Clark, Oakland Hill, CA; 10 M. Harpur/ Park Farm, Great Waltham, Essex; 10–11 J. Harpur/Sharon Drusch, Del Mar, CA; 11 left J. Harpur/Molly Chapellet, Napa Valley, CA; 11 right J. Harpur/House of Pitmuies, Angus, Scotland; 12 M. Harpur/Mr & Mrs Colin McKay, Norfolk; 13 M. Harpur/Beth Chatto Gardens, Essex; 14 J. Harpur/Dr & Mrs Chris Grey-Wilson, Suffolk; 15 J. Harpur; 16 top M. Harpur/Old Rectory, Sudborough, Northants; 16 below J. Harpur; 17 J. Harpur/Manor House, Heslington, Yorkshire; 18 M. Harpur/Holkham Hall, Wells-next-the-Sea, Norfolk; 19 left J. Harpur/Dolwen, Powys; 19 right M. Harpur/ Old Rectory, Sudborough, Northants; 20 left J. Harpur/Manor House, Bledlow, Bucks; 20 right J. Harpur; 21 J. Harpur/RHS Rosemoor, Devon; 22 J. Harpur; 23 clockwise from top left: J. Harpur/RHS Wisley, Surrey; J. Harpur; J. Harpur; J. Harpur/RHS Wisley, Surrey; J. Harpur; M. Harpur; J. Harpur/RHS Wisley, Surrey; 24 J. Harpur/Rofford Manor, Oxfordshire; 25 J. Harpur/Beth Chatto Gardens, Essex; 26 J. Harpur; 27 left J. Harpur; 27 right J. Harpur; 28 left J. Harpur; 28 right J. Harpur; 29 left J. Harpur; 29 right M. Harpur/Chenies Manor, Buckinghamshire; 30 J. Harpur/design: Dan Hinkley, Seattle; 31 top left J. Harpur; 31 top right J. Harpur; 31 below J. Harpur/ design: Linda Cochran, Washington; 32 J. Harpur; 32–33 J. Harpur; 33 J. Harpur; 34 J. Harpur; 35 clockwise from top left: J. Harpur; J. Harpur/design: C. Price & G. Witty, Seattle; Andrew Lawson; Andrew Lawson; Andrew Lawson; Andrew Lawson; J. Harpur; 36 J. Harpur/Wyevale, Chelsea Flower Show; 37 J. Harpur; 38 left J. Harpur/Manor House, Heslington, Yorkshire; 38 right J. Harpur; 39 J. Harpur/design: Dr James Smart, Marwood Hill, Devon; 40 J. Harpur/design: Dr James Smart, Marwood Hill, Devon; 40–41 M. Harpur/Glen Chantry, Essex; 41 top J. Harpur; 41 below J. Harpur/ Great Dixter, East Sussex; 42 J. Harpur; 43 clockwise from top left: J. Harpur; J. Harpur; J. Harpur; J. Harpur; Andrew Lawson; Andrew Lawson; 44 J. Harpur/Beth Chatto Gardens, Essex; 45 M. Harpur/ Beth Chatto Gardens, Essex; 46 left M. Harpur/Mr & Mrs Colin McKay, Norfolk; 46 right J. Harpur/Stone House Cottage, Worcestershire; 47 M. Harpur/Holkham Hall, Wells-next-the-Sea, Norfolk; 48 left M. Harpur/Holkham Hall, Wells-next-the-Sea, Norfolk; 48 right J. Harpur/RHS Wisley, Surrey; 49 left J. Harpur/ Beth Chatto Gardens, Essex; 49 right Andrew Lawson; 50 left M. Harpur/Holkham Hall, Wells-next-the-Sea, Norfolk; 50 right J. Harpur; 51 J. Harpur; 52–53 M. Harpur; 54 J. Harpur; 55 clockwise from top left: J. Harpur; J. Harpur; J. Harpur; Andrew Lawson; J. Harpur; M. Harpur; J. Harpur; J. Harpur; 56 M. Harpur/Mr & Mrs Colin McKay, Norfolk; 57 J. Harpur/ Beth Chatto Gardens, Essex; 58 left Andrew Lawson; 58 right J. Harpur; 59 J. Harpur/Peter Wooster, Roxbury, Conn. USA; 60 left J. Harpur; 60 right J. Harpur/Beth Chatto Gardens, Essex; 60–61 J. Harpur/design: Gunilla Pickard, Fanners Green, Essex; 61 right M. Harpur/Mr & Mrs Colin McKay, Norfolk; 62 left J. Harpur/design: Dan Hinkley, Seattle; 62–63 Andrew Lawson/Chilcombe House, Dorset; 63 J. Harpur; 64 M. Harpur; 65 clockwise from top left: J. Harpur; J. Harpur; J. Harpur/ Beth Chatto Gardens, Essex; Andrew Lawson; Jerry Harpur; J. Harpur; J. Harpur; 66 J. Harpur/design: R. Hartlage, Seattle; 67 J. Harpur; 68 left J. Harpur; 68 right J. Harpur; 69 Andrew Lawson; 70 left Andrew Lawson; 70–71 Andrew Lawson; 71 Andrew Lawson; 72–73 above Andrew Lawson; 72–73 below M. Harpur/Old Rectory, Sudborough, Northants; 73 centre J. Harpur; 73 below J. Harpur; 74 J. Harpur; 75 clockwise from top left: J. Harpur; J. Harpur; J. Harpur; J. Harpur; Andrew Lawson; J. Harpur; J. Harpur; 77 M. Harpur; 80 J. Harpur.